# Discover the Saints

This book
belongs to:

_____

_____

---

The content in this program was developed and reviewed by the content engagement team at Saint Mary's Press. Content design and manufacturing were coordinated by the passionate team of creatives at Saint Mary's Press.

Saint artwork created by © Vicki Shuck/Saint Mary's Press.

Printed in the United States of America

5045 (PO6425)

978-1-64121-079-9

saint mary's press

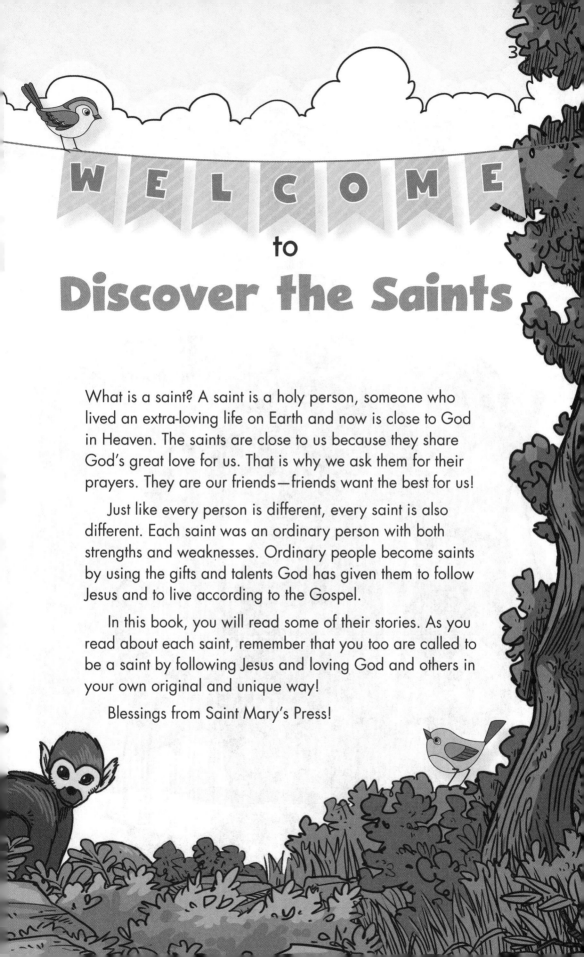

# WELCOME

## to

# Discover the Saints

What is a saint? A saint is a holy person, someone who lived an extra-loving life on Earth and now is close to God in Heaven. The saints are close to us because they share God's great love for us. That is why we ask them for their prayers. They are our friends—friends want the best for us!

Just like every person is different, every saint is also different. Each saint was an ordinary person with both strengths and weaknesses. Ordinary people become saints by using the gifts and talents God has given them to follow Jesus and to live according to the Gospel.

In this book, you will read some of their stories. As you read about each saint, remember that you too are called to be a saint by following Jesus and loving God and others in your own original and unique way!

Blessings from Saint Mary's Press!

# Saint Elizabeth Ann Seton

(1774–1821)

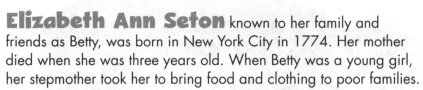

**Elizabeth Ann Seton** known to her family and friends as Betty, was born in New York City in 1774. Her mother died when she was three years old. When Betty was a young girl, her stepmother took her to bring food and clothing to poor families. When Betty was older, she started a society to help poor mothers and children.

Betty married William M. Seton in 1794, and they lived happily with their five children until William became ill. The family thought that a trip to Italy would help him heal. Yet he died shortly after their arrival.

While in Italy, Betty went to Mass with her Catholic friends and learned that Jesus was really and truly present in the Eucharist. Returning to New York, she studied the Catholic faith and was received into the Church. When she started a school for girls in Baltimore, several young women joined her. They began the Sisters of Charity—a community dedicated to educating poor children. From then on, Betty became known as Mother Seton.

Mother Seton died in 1821. She is the first native-born American saint and is recognized for beginning the Catholic school system in the United States.

## Prayer

**Saint Elizabeth Ann Seton**, you met the challenges of your life with courage and faith. Pray to God for me, that I may be strong and courageous too.

**Write a prayer asking God, through the prayers of Saint Elizabeth Ann Seton, to bless your favorite teacher.**

SCHOOL

Feast Day
January
**21**

**Agnes** was only twelve years old when she became a martyr, a person who died for her faith. It happened something like this:

Agnes was brought up in a faithful Christian family. At that time, Christians had to remain hidden because Christianity was outlawed in the Roman Empire. Agnes received many proposals of marriage, but declined them all, preferring to be free to dedicate her life to Christ. It is thought that one of her suitors (someone who is asking for marriage) denounced her as a Christian and handed in her name to the Roman authorities.

The name Agnes means "pure" and sounds a lot like the Latin word *agnus*, which means "lamb." This is why Agnes is often pictured holding a lamb. The lamb reminds us of Jesus, the Lamb of God, for whom Agnes gave her life. Saint Agnes is honored as the patron saint of girls.

## Prayer

**Saint Agnes**, ask God to help me make good choices in freedom, love, and peace.

Write a prayer asking Saint Agnes to pray for a girl you know. You might choose a girl who needs extra help at this time.

# Saint John Bosco

**(1815–1888)**

Feast Day
January
**31**

**John Bosco** was born to a farming family in Italy. He was a fun-loving boy, and he used his fun-loving ways to teach other children about God. He put on shows for the neighborhood children. He did magic tricks, juggled, and walked the tightrope. The "ticket" to the show was one Rosary, recited by the spectators on the spot! At the very end, John would repeat the parish priest's Sunday sermon for all to hear!

When John grew up, he became a priest. He founded religious communities of both men and women to work with him in teaching and helping children, and he had special concern for the young boys he found living on the streets. He gave these boys a home and prepared them to live good and honest lives through education and work training. Saint John is now honored as the patron saint of young people.

## Prayer

**Saint John Bosco**, pray for me, so that I may use my gifts and talents to bring the love of God to others. Amen.

**How can you use your gifts and talents to bring joy and love to others? Share your thoughts with Saint John Bosco below.**

# Saint Katharine Drexel (1858–1955)

Stand up for justice and fairness.

**Katharine Drexel** and her sisters were brought up in a good and generous Catholic family near Philadelphia. Katharine learned that money should be used to help others. She was especially aware of the unfair treatment faced by black Americans and of the desperate needs of Native Americans.

When Katharine's father died, Katharine received a fortune: millions of dollars. But she knew that money alone would not solve the problems she had seen. When she met with Pope Leo XIII, she asked him to send missionaries to black and Native Americans in the United States. (*Missionaries* are people who spread the Good News of the Gospel by preaching and helping those in need.)

"My daughter," responded the pope, "Why not go yourself?" Katharine decided to form a religious community. She named her community the Sisters of the Blessed Sacrament.

Mother Katharine used her fortune to found schools and missions for black and Native Americans. She also founded Xavier University in New Orleans especially for black Americans.

Saint Katharine Drexel is the patron saint of racial justice and philanthropists (those who give money to good causes).

## Prayer

**Saint Katharine Drexel**, ask God to give me your concern for liberty and justice for all.

Ask Saint Katharine to pray that you will be generous with your time, talent, or treasure! What good cause can you support? Write its name or draw a picture of it here.

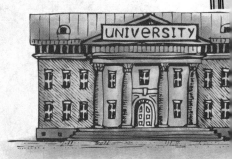

# Saint Patrick

(c. 389–461)

Feast Day
March
**17**

**Patrick** was first brought to Ireland as a slave and worked as a shepherd boy. Before his escape six years later, Patrick came to admire the Irish people. Back home again, he had a dream. He dreamed he heard the voice of the Irish: "Patrick, come and walk among us!" Patrick became a priest. He went back to Ireland to bring the true faith to the Irish people. It was Patrick who lit the first Easter fire in Ireland to announce the Resurrection of Christ.

Patrick became a bishop. The shepherd boy became the chief spiritual shepherd and teacher of the Irish people. It is said that Patrick first explained the Holy Trinity by holding up a shamrock with its three leaves. In both the fire and the shamrock, Patrick announced that new light and new life had come to Ireland—the light and life of Christ!

**Ireland**

## Prayer

**Saint Patrick**, pray for me, that I might spread the light and life of Christ to everyone I meet.

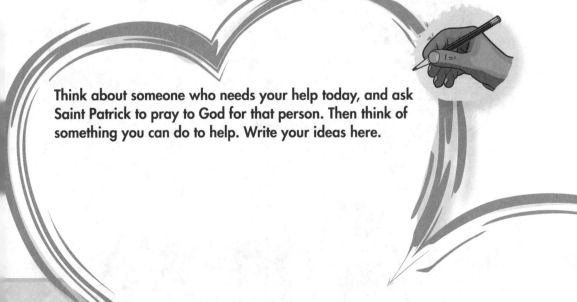

Think about someone who needs your help today, and ask Saint Patrick to pray to God for that person. Then think of something you can do to help. Write your ideas here.

Feast Day
March
**19**

**Joseph** is the foster father of Jesus and the husband of Mary. We also know Joseph as "the silent saint" because not one word spoken by Joseph is recorded in the Gospels. Jesus, dying on the cross, gave the care of his mother to the Apostle John, and so we think that Joseph must have already died. Because he probably died in the presence of Mary and Jesus, we call Saint Joseph "the patron of a happy death."

Saint Joseph also has another title: the Patron of the Universal Church. Because Saint Joseph took such good care of Mary and Jesus, he also takes good care of the Church. As he once held the tiny body of the infant Jesus, he now holds the Church in his arms.

Because Joseph was a carpenter and probably made furniture for homes, people ask his prayers for any needs they have in regard to their own homes, especially when they are buying or selling a home.

## Prayer

**Saint Joseph**, as you watched over Jesus, pray to God for me and watch over me.

**Saint Joseph was a family man. Take some time to write a prayer to Saint Joseph, asking him to pray to God for your needs and the needs of your family. Name some of these needs.**

# Saint
# John Baptist de La Salle
(1651–1719)

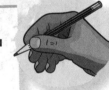
Feast Day
April
7

## John Baptist de La Salle would be the first to tell you that he never intended to create a religious community! He was headed for a quiet priestly life. However, when he became concerned about boys roaming the streets all day, his life changed.

At that time, education was given by tutors, one-on-one. Parents who worked for a living could not afford tutors. Father John said, "Let's group the boys together and offer education free of charge." He invited the teachers (all men) to live with him in his home. This was the beginning of the Brothers of the Christian Schools, or Lasallian Brothers.

Father John taught that teaching is a vocation, a calling from God. The teachers included religion in their teaching, and helped the boys learn skills that would serve them well in everyday life. Father John's system became the normal method of educating children. Saint John Baptist de La Salle is the patron saint of all those who work in the field of education.

Saint John Baptist de La Salle has two feast days! We celebrate his feast day on April 7. In Lasallian schools, he is also remembered and celebrated on May 15, Founder's Day.

## Prayer

**Saint John Baptist de La Salle**, pray for me. Ask God to help me do my best in school and to value my education.

**How do you feel about school? Write to Saint John Baptist de La Salle. Ask him to pray for you. Talk to him about any problems you may have in school.**

# Saint Catherine of Siena (1347–1380)

Follow **Jesus** – and set the world on fire!

Feast Day
April
**29**

## Catherine of Siena knew one thing for sure.

The Pope did not belong in France. In 1309, a French pope had been elected but refused to move to Rome, so popes lived in France for the next sixty-seven years! But Catherine knew that Rome was not just any other city. Rome was the "See (or seat of authority) of Peter," the first Pope, and a sign of unity. The Pope belonged in Rome. Catherine wrote to Pope Gregory XI many times, and even visited him in France. She asked him to return to Rome as a sign of unity with the entire Church. And he did, in 1376.

Even during her lifetime, Catherine was considered a holy person and a woman who made a difference. A gifted writer and teacher, she was surrounded by a group of disciples who looked to her for guidance in living the Christian life.

Saint Catherine was one of two women named a Doctor of the Church by Pope Paul VI in 1970. Because of her writings and her powerful letters, Catherine is the patron saint of journalists, the media, and the communication professions.

### Prayer

**Saint Catherine of Siena**, ask God to help me to "speak truth to power."

Saint Catherine's letters made a difference. Write a letter to someone about something you would like to see changed. Who will you write to? What will you say? Use this space for your rough draft.

# Saint Dominic Savio
### (1842–1857)

Feast Day
May
6

**Dominic Savio** was twelve years old when he became a student of another saint, Saint John Bosco. Dominic wanted to be a priest and to help his teacher in working with homeless boys. Dominic loved playground time as much as anyone else, and he often helped to break up fights and to make peace. Yet he also had a gift for prayer, and he stopped to pray often, wherever he was—even on the playground. He organized a special group of students who helped John Bosco with the boys and with manual work around the school. The members of this group became the first members of the congregation that John Bosco created to carry on his work.

Dominic did not have good health and had to be sent home from school. His health did not improve at home, and, after receiving the Sacrament of Anointing of the Sick and Holy Communion, he died at the age of fourteen. His teacher, John Bosco, wrote an account of Dominic's life, and Dominic was made a saint in 1954.

## Prayer

**Saint Dominic Savio**, pray for me, that I may do little things cheerfully.

Saint Dominic Savio was a peacemaker and helper in his school. How can you become a peacemaker and helper in your school or family? Write your ideas here.

# Saint Joan of Arc

(1045–1093)

Feast Day
May
**30**

**Joan of Arc** was a young French girl of sixteen when she heard the voices of Saint Michael, Saint Catherine, and Saint Margaret. The French and the English were at war, and the voices were asking her to drive the English out of France and to bring Prince Charles, the heir to the French throne, to Reims for his coronation as king.

When Joan arrived at the French court, she met with Prince Charles. She did not carry a weapon, but only a banner bearing the names of Jesus and Mary. Joan's mission was successful. The prince was crowned king and the French army won battle after battle. Then Joan was captured and tried in court as a heretic and a witch. She was given no legal help, was found guilty, and was burned at the stake in 1431. At the end of the war, her trial was reviewed, and the court declared Joan innocent on July 7, 1456. Joan of Arc is the patron saint of France and of members of the military.

## Prayer

**Saint Joan of Arc**, pray for me, that I may keep the names of Jesus and Mary close to me, as you did.

Flag of France

**Saint Joan of Arc once said that she would have liked to have stayed at home, helping her mother, rather than go to war. But this was God's will for her. What hard things have you or your family been asked to do? Write a prayer asking Saint Joan's help in doing God's will.**

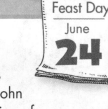
Feast Day
June
**24**

**John the Baptist** was a cousin of Jesus. Jesus probably had other cousins, but John is the most famous. John was called "the Baptizer" because he announced the coming of Jesus to the world, and offered a baptism of repentance to prepare for Jesus' coming. He even baptized Jesus himself!

John the Baptist did not hesitate to call out the sins of King Herod of Judea, and so Herod had him beheaded. After John was killed, Jesus began preaching about the Kingdom of God. John had prepared the way, and it was Jesus' turn to carry God's message to the world.

At Mass we pray "Lamb of God, who takes away the sins of the world, have mercy on us" *(Roman Missal)*. We can thank John the Baptist for this prayer, who pointed out Jesus as "the Lamb of God."

## Prayer

**Saint John the Baptist**, thank you for giving your life to prepare the world for Jesus. Ask God to help me prepare to meet Jesus each day in his Word, his sacraments, and in love.

Saint John the Baptist knew that it was important to prepare to meet Jesus. How do you prepare to meet Jesus in Holy Communion? in those around you? in those in need?

# Saints Peter and Paul

(first century)

**Peter and Paul** are called "the pillars of the Church." This tells us how important they are. How important are pillars? There is a saying among builders: "No roof, no house." But something very important holds up the roof, and those are the pillars. You can see round or square pillars holding up roofs everywhere. From the beginning, Peter and Paul have held up the Church and so provided shelter for the entire People of God!

Saint Peter was chosen by Jesus to be the leader of the Apostles. Peter was the first Pope and Bishop of Rome, and since then the Catholic Church has been led by his successors. Saint Paul was chosen by Jesus to turn from persecuting the Church to helping it grow. Each had an important mission to accomplish in the early Church. Each gave his life as a martyr. They share the same feast day because they shared equally in spreading the Good News of Jesus Christ throughout the world.

In this picture, Saint Paul is writing a letter. To whom is the letter addressed? Turn the picture upside down to see!

## Prayer

**Saints Peter and Paul**, ask God to help me to cooperate with others in spreading the Good News of Jesus.

**Jesus did not choose Peter or Paul because they were perfect. He chose them because they could listen and change. What change can you make to follow Jesus more closely?**

# Saint Kateri Tekakwitha
### (1656–1680)

Care for the **Earth** and pray to God in your **heart**.

**Feast Day**
July
**14**

**Kateri Tekakwitha** was born in what is now upstate New York. Her mother was a Christian Algonquin, and her father was a Mohawk chief. When she was four, a smallpox epidemic took both her parents and her little brother. She was left scarred and half-blind. (Her name, Tekakwitha, means "she who bumps into things.") She was adopted by her uncle, who had no love for Christians but was required by treaty to allow the presence of "black robes" (Jesuit missionaries) in his village. Kateri refused marriage and was baptized at age nineteen on Easter Sunday. She was given the name Kateri, or Catherine.

At the advice of a priest, Kateri left her village, on foot, for a Christian village in Canada, two hundred miles away! She lived an ordinary life, seeking out quiet places in the woods where she could pray. Kateri is the patron saint of ecology and the environment, people in exile, and Native Americans.

## Prayer

**Saint Kateri**, pray for me, that I too may find God in my ordinary life.

Name some ways you or your family can care for the environment. Use the five Rs as guidelines: reduce, reuse, recycle, repair, refuse (for example, refuse to use unnecessary plastic, or opt out of junk mail lists to save paper).

# Saint
# Mary Magdalene
(first century)

Feast Day
July
**22**

**Mary Magdalene** was a faithful disciple of Jesus. After Jesus was buried in the tomb, Mary came to the tomb while it was still dark. She looked into the tomb and did not find the body of Jesus. She stood at the tomb, crying. But when she turned around, she saw someone she thought was the gardener and asked him where the body of Jesus was. That gardener said, "Mary!" and Mary Magdalene suddenly knew that this was not the gardener, but the Risen Jesus. Mary responded, "Teacher!" Then she did as Jesus told her. She went and told the disciples that Jesus had risen from the dead. For this reason, Mary Magdalene is called "the Apostle to the Apostles."

## Prayer

**Saint Mary Magdalene**, pray for me, that I may follow Jesus as my true Teacher.

Write down some things you have learned from Jesus, your Teacher.

# Saint Clare of Assisi

(1193–1253)

**Feast Day**
August
**11**

**Saint Clare of Assisi** was born into a noble family of Assisi. When she was eighteen years old, she heard Francis of Assisi preach. She immediately knew that she wanted to live the Gospel way of life that he lived. Knowing that her parents would not approve, she slipped away one night. She met Francis in a little chapel. He cut off her long hair and gave her a plain robe and veil to wear. Eventually other women joined her (including her sisters and, later, her mother) and thus began the Franciscan order now known as the Poor Clares.

Saint Clare wrote a rule, or way of life, for her monastery, the first ever written by a woman. The sisters were to live in strict poverty, as Jesus did, and were to be supported by their own work and by begging. The sisters helped their Franciscan brothers by prayer and encouragement. Clare took care of Francis during his last illness. Clare's chosen way to live the Gospel makes clear that both prayer and action are necessary in following Jesus.

## Prayer

**Saint Clare of Assisi**, pray for me, that I may follow in the footsteps of Jesus.

**Look around your house or your room. Write down some things you have that you really don't use or need. Then circle something that you can give to someone in need. Make a plan to do it!**

DONATE

# Pope
# Saint Pius X

(1835–1914)

Love Jesus and **receive** Holy Communion often.

**Pope Pius X** was born Giuseppe (Joseph) Sarto. His father was a postman. The family, though poor, valued education, and Giuseppe walked almost 4 miles to school and back every day! He was first in his class in grammar school, in high school, and in seminary. When he became Pope, he would often escape the papal palace and visit the sick in hospitals. He made a habit of carrying candy with him so that he could give treats to the children he met on the streets.

Pope Pius's motto was "To restore all things in Christ." He made changes to some Church practices. For example, he refused to be carried into Saint Peter's Basilica on a chair high above the people, but walked in procession like everyone else. In his concern for earthquake victims, he opened the papal palace to them, long before the Italian government offered any help.

Pope Pius X required every parish to offer religious instruction to children, encouraged daily Mass and Communion for all Catholics, and lowered the age for receiving First Communion from twelve to seven. For this reason, he has been declared the patron saint of First Communicants.

## Prayer

**Pope Saint Pius X**, thank you for your care for children and for the sick. Ask God to give me the grace of caring for those who are in special need.

# GET WELL SOON

Copy your parish sick list in this space. Pray for each person on the list. If possible, send a get-well card (through your parish secretary or minister to the homebound) to each person.

# Saint Mother Teresa of Kolkata
## (Calcutta) (1910–1997)

Do something **beautiful** for God!

**Feast Day**
September
**5**

**Mother Teresa** is famous worldwide for her service to the "poorest of the poor." She even won the Nobel Peace Prize for her work. Even before her death, many people believed she was a saint.

But Mother Teresa was not always famous. She was born in the small country of North Macedonia (part of the former Yugoslavia). When she was eighteen, she entered the Sisters of Loreto in Ireland in hopes of becoming a missionary. That dream came true when she was sent to India. She taught in a school for girls in Kolkata for nearly twenty years. While on a train trip to her annual retreat, Mother Teresa received her "call within a call": to leave her convent but remain a sister and work directly with the poor.

For her religious habit, she wore a white sari (the ordinary dress of Indian women) with a blue border. She began tending to the poor, the sick, and the hungry. Young women joined her, and together they became the Missionaries of Charity. Mother Teresa's little community now numbers over 4,500 sisters worldwide, with many other helpers and associates.

## Prayer

**India**

**Saint Mother Teresa**, ask God to show me how to help those who are poor, especially those in my town or city.

**Saint Mother Teresa often remarked that the loneliest people can be found right around us, in our own families. Write down the names of your family members, along with something special you can do with or for each one this week.**

# Saint Thérèse of Lisieux

(1873–1897)

**Thérèse of Lisieux** was a very sensitive child. Her feelings were always getting hurt. Her mother and sisters taught her to offer up her small difficulties to Jesus. Gradually she learned to rise above her sensitive feelings. When she asked to enter the Carmelite monastery at age fifteen, both the nuns and her local bishop refused to admit her. On a pilgrimage to Rome with her family, she broke through the crowd, stood before the Pope, and asked *his* permission! Everyone admired her courage, and she was allowed to enter the monastery.

In the monastery, Sister Thérèse taught the sisters what she called her "Little Way": doing little things for Jesus and helping others even when it is hard. She saw herself as a "little flower" in God's garden—not big and strong like the roses, but like a little wildflower that sometimes gets stepped on but pops right up again.

Before her death, she wrote her life story, *The Story of a Soul*, which became popular all over the world. Her "Little Way" helped many others to follow Jesus in their ordinary lives. The rose is her special sign of her love and prayers.

## Prayer

**Saint Thérèse of Lisieux**, ask Jesus to show me how to live your "Little Way" in my everyday life.

**Saint Thérèse offered her prayer for missionaries, those who spread the Good News to others, especially to people in other countries. Write down the name of a group who does this. (Or perhaps your parish has a "sister parish" in another country.) Keep that group or parish in your prayers each day this week.**

**Théodore Guérin** arrived in Indiana in October of 1840 with five other sisters from France and asked to visit the Blessed Sacrament. The sisters were shocked that they were led to a one-room log cabin in the midst of a forest! The sisters were used to the beautiful cathedrals of Europe. They had never seen the Blessed Sacrament kept in a log cabin before!

Then the sisters were led to the attic of a wooden house, where a farm family was already living on the first floor. They spent their first winter in America there. Snow drifted in through the wooden boards in the roof. But even before the sisters built their own convent, they built a sturdy brick school. That school became Saint Mary-of-the-Woods College. Sister Théodore became known as Mother Théodore, foundress of the Sisters of Providence of Saint Mary-of-the-Woods. Soon the sisters were opening schools all over the Midwest.

Mother Théodore taught her sisters and her students to trust in God's providence, God's loving care for his children, whether they lived in a beautiful palace or in a log cabin in the middle of a forest.

## Prayer

**Saint Mother Théodore**, ask God to help me trust in his loving care for me.

**God's loving care (providence) often comes through the kindness of others. How can you be God's loving care for someone in need this week? Write down your ideas.**

# Saint Francis of Assisi (c. 1181–1226)

**Francis of Assisi** has been called the most beloved saint of all time. Why is that? Perhaps because he was full of love and joy. He loved people (especially those who were poor). He loved the natural world. He loved animals, both wild and tame. He was full of love!

But Francis was not always like this. When he was a young man, he thought only of spending his father's money on good times with his friends. Yet he wanted to do better. One day, while Francis prayed before a crucifix in the Church of San Damiano, Christ spoke to him. Christ asked Francis to repair his house, meaning the Church. But Francis took this to mean the little church of San Damiano! He began repairing the ruined stone church.

After hearing the Gospel in which Christ told his disciples to go and proclaim the Kingdom, Francis did just that. He began to preach and to devote himself to poverty, wearing a simple robe and a knotted belt. The people listened to him because he lived what he preached. Young men joined him, and so began the Franciscan Order. Saint Francis is honored as the patron saint of animals and the environment.

## Prayer

**Saint Francis**, ask God to fill me with love and joy!

**Francis respected the natural world as a gift from God. In each box below, write something you will do to show respect for the environment. Draw an X over the box when you have taken each action.**

Medal
of
FREEDOM

**Pope John XXIII** was Pope for only four years, but what a difference he made to the Church and to the world! Pope John sensed that the Catholic Church needed a time of renewal, and so, inspired by the Holy Spirit, he called the Second Vatican Council. He invited bishops from the Eastern Orthodox Churches and pastors from Protestant churches and faith communities as observers. Many decisions made by this council still shape our lives as Catholics today.

As a priest and bishop, the future Pope was sent to many other countries and served many different kinds of people. During World War II, by working and talking with various governments, he rescued and arranged for the safety of many Jewish individuals, families, and children.

Above all, Pope John XXIII worked for peace. For his efforts, the United States awarded him its highest civilian award, the Presidential Medal of Freedom. On the medal is inscribed: "He brought to all citizens of the planet a heightened sense of the dignity of the individual, of the brotherhood of man, and of the common duty to build an environment of peace for all humankind." Pope Saint John XXIII's feast day is October 11, the day that the Second Vatican Council opened.

## Prayer

**Pope Saint John XXIII**, ask Jesus to show me the way to peace each day.

Think about what peace means to you—in your life, in your family, in your world. Draw a picture or symbol that shows this meaning of peace.

**Teresa of Ávila** and her brother decided to become martyrs at a young age. (Martyrs are those who die for their beliefs.) One morning they left home for a foreign land, but were found along the road by an uncle, who brought them back to their family. When Teresa grew up, she found another way to witness to God's love.

Teresa became a nun in a monastery for women. At first she was not a very good nun. But as she began to pray more regularly, she began receiving messages from Jesus. He called her to begin a new monastery, where the nuns could be more serious about prayer. But Teresa believed in a balanced life too. She made sure to put recreation time into the daily schedule, and often played the tambourine for the nuns so they could dance!

Saint Teresa was made a Doctor of the Church because of her writings on prayer. Saint Teresa believed that prayer is possible, no matter what we are doing, because prayer is a matter of love. She said, "Know that even when you are in the kitchen, our Lord is moving amidst the pots and pans."

## Prayer

**Saint Teresa of Ávila**, ask Jesus to help me to find him everywhere.

How we feel and act depends on how we think. Write down some loving thoughts to remember when you are feeling angry or upset. For example: "Jesus, help me"; "Lord, have mercy"; "The Lord is my shepherd."

**Pope John Paul II** was a young man in Poland when Germany invaded his country and began World War II. Churches and religious houses were closed. Jews were sent away to labor camps or to certain death. In the midst of these evils, a young man named Karol Wojtyla decided to become a priest. He had to study for the priesthood in secret.

As a priest, Father Wojtyla formed a group of about twenty young people, and they gathered for prayer, discussion, and to give help to the poor. The group grew to about two hundred, and their activities included annual skiing and kayaking trips. When Karol Wojtyla became Pope John Paul II, he sometimes took an afternoon off to ski!

Pope John Paul II became one of our most beloved popes. He reached out to those of other religions in prayers for unity and peace. He included young people in the life of the Church by beginning World Youth Day. When he was shot by a young man in Saint Peter's Square, he visited the young man in prison and forgave him.

As he lay near death, thousands of people filled Saint Peter's Square for two days, carrying candles and singing hymns. The Pope could hear the singing and said, "I thank you."

## Prayer

**Pope Saint John Paul II**, pray for me, that I may know Christ and his power in my life.

We may never have to face the difficult times that Pope Saint John Paul II faced. But Jesus cares for us and wants to help us in our own difficult times. Write a prayer asking Pope Saint John Paul II to pray for you in your difficult times.

# Saint Martin de Porres

(1579-1639)

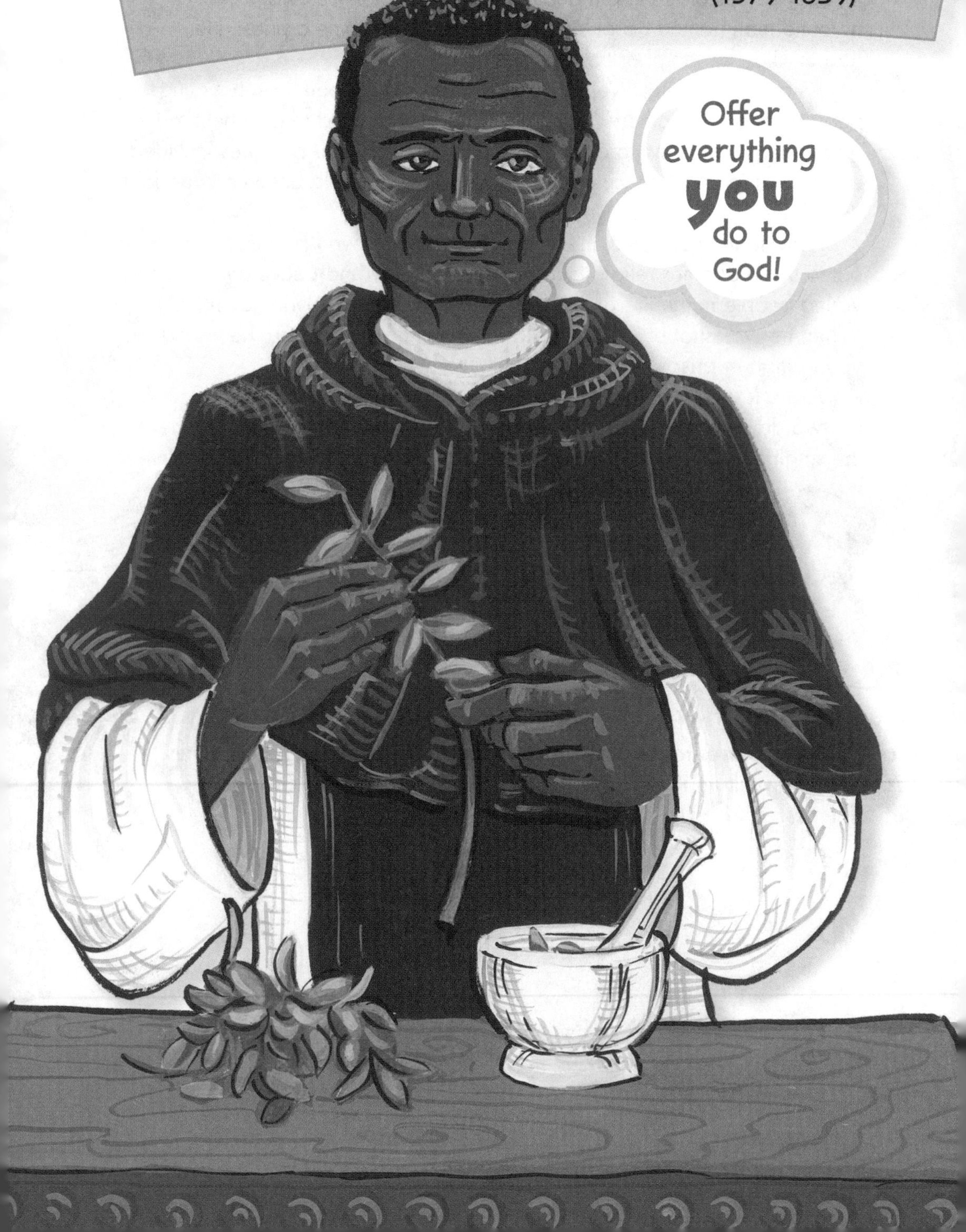

**Martin de Porres** was born in Lima, Peru. He inherited the features and dark complexion of his mother, who was from Panama. His father, originally from Spain, disliked his son's looks. After Martin's sister was born, his father abandoned the family and left Martin's mother to raise the two children alone. In childhood and even as an adult, Martin was mocked for being of mixed race.

When Martin was twelve, he went to work for a barber. He not only learned to cut hair but also to use various herbs to help the sick. He joined the Dominican order as a "lay helper," but after a few years, the community asked him to join as a vowed member. Martin oversaw almsgiving (helping the poor with money and goods), as well as taking care of the sick. His concern extended to animals, and he founded the first animal shelter in the New World (the lands across the ocean from Europe) at his sister's farm. Martin is the patron saint of those seeking racial harmony.

## Prayer

**Saint Martin de Porres**, pray for me, that I may treat everyone I meet with kindness.

**Saint Martin de Porres was looked down on because he was different. Write a prayer here for those who are teased or bullied.**

**Feast Day**
**November**
**17**

**Elizabeth of Hungary** was born a princess, the daughter of the king of Hungary. She married Louis of Thuringia (Germany), and together they had three children Elizabeth could have lived a life of luxury, but she chose to live simply and to devote herself to the poor and to the sick. Rather than spend money on extravagant clothing, Elizabeth chose to spend the resources of the palace on food for the hungry. When her husband died, his family threw her out of the palace, accusing her of wasting the royal family's money. However, she was allowed back into the palace when her husband's friends returned from war, because her son was the legal heir to the throne.

Elizabeth joined the Franciscan Third Order (now called the Secular Franciscans) and served in a hospital she herself had commanded to be built. At her death, many healings were reported due to her prayers and so she was canonized only four years later. She is the patron saint of nurses, charitable organizations, and homeless people.

## Prayer

**Saint Elizabeth of Hungary**, pray for me, that I may never forget to help those who are poor or sick.

Ask Saint Elizabeth of Hungary to pray for those in hospitals or retirement centers and their caregivers. Write down the names of the hospitals and retirement centers near you. Pray for the doctors, nurses, aides, and patients (or residents) in each one.

Feast Day
November
**22**

**Cecilia** is the patron saint of musicians, and she is often pictured playing a harpsichord (an early version of an organ) or a small lyre (as in this picture), or carrying a small set of pipes with a keyboard.

Cecilia had vowed her life to Christ, but her parents forced her to marry. During the wedding, while the musicians were playing, it is said that Cecilia sang in her heart to God.

Cecilia convinced her husband, Valerian, to become a Christian. Both Valerian and his brother were martyred, and then Cecilia was martyred as well. Before she died, she asked that her home be converted into a church. That church is now called Saint Cecilia in Trastevere, in Rome. This is where her body was buried and where she is still honored today.

## Prayer

**Saint Cecilia**, pray for me, that I may always sing to God in my heart.

Ask Saint Cecilia to pray for all musicians, and especially for the musicians, cantors, and singers in your parish who help your parish assembly to celebrate the Eucharist. Name your parish and the Mass time you and your family usually attend. Draw some instruments you see in church.

# Saint
# Francis Xavier
## (1506–1552)

**Francis Xavier** was born to a well-to-do family in the Kingdom of Navarre (later taken over by Spain) and met Saint Ignatius Loyola when both were studying in Paris. With five other friends, they took religious vows and began the Society of Jesus (the Jesuits). Francis was sent to spread the Catholic faith in India when the priest originally chosen for this mission fell ill. When he reached India, Francis began to minister to the sick. Then he reached out to the children as he walked through the streets, ringing a bell to announce his lessons about Jesus. Francis's missionary journeys later took him from India to Japan and Borneo. He was about to enter China when he died on a nearby island.

Francis Xavier is called "Apostle to the Indies" and "Apostle of Japan." Together with Saint Thérèse of Lisieux, he is honored as the patron saint of missionaries.

## Prayer

**Saint Francis Xavier**, pray for me, that I may share my faith, hope, and love with others.

Choose a missionary society or other agency that serves people outside the United States. Write the name of this group here, and write a prayer asking Saint Francis Xavier to pray for the people they serve. If possible, send a donation to this group.

**Juan Diego,** a native Mexican Indian, was hurrying to Mass along a path on Tepeyac Hill (near Mexico City). Suddenly he saw a beautiful woman. The woman told him that she was Mary, the Mother of God. She asked him to go to the bishop and ask that a shrine be built in her honor on this very hill. Juan Diego did as Mary asked, but the bishop asked for a sign.

The next time Juan Diego met Mary, she asked him to collect some of the flowers growing on the hillside. (Flowers did not usually grow there in December!) Mary arranged the flowers in Juan Diego's cloak. When he met with the bishop again, Juan Diego opened his cloak. The bishop saw the flowers, and something else too: a beautiful image of Our Lady imprinted on the cloak!

The Shrine of Our Lady of Guadalupe was built, and the image of Our Lady on the cloak remains on display there still today. People still come to see it and ask for Mary's prayers for themselves and their loved ones.

Juan Diego remained the humble, quiet person that he always was. He spent the rest of his days living near the shrine, grateful for his small part in Mary's plan to show her motherly love for her children.

## Prayer

**Saint Juan Diego,** pray to God for me, that I may do the next good thing God asks of me.

A shrine is a special place of prayer. Make one in your home, using a crucifix or a picture of Mary or Jesus. Write your prayer requests here, and spend time praying at your shrine.

# Saint John the Apostle
### (first century)

Feast Day
December
**27**

**John the Apostle** was the youngest of all the Apostles, and he lived the longest. He is called "the beloved disciple" because he is described as "the one whom Jesus loved" (John 13:23). As Jesus was dying on the cross, he entrusted the care of his mother, Mary, to John.

According to tradition, Saint John the Apostle wrote the fourth Gospel, the Gospel of John, and the first of three Letters of John. During a persecution of Christians, John was exiled to the Island of Patmos in Greece. There he received several visions, which he wrote down in what is now known as the Book of Revelation. This is the last book in the Bible. It is called Revelation because it reveals, or shows, the truth about our life here on Earth and the life to come in Heaven. The Book of Revelation encourages us to stay faithful, because Christ has already won the victory for us, the victory over sin and death.

It is said that when John was a very old man, he said one simple phrase over and over: "Little children, love one another." Perhaps this is why Saint John is known as "the Apostle of Love."

## Prayer

**Saint John the Apostle**, ask Jesus to help me be his true friend and a true friend to others.

Saint John is called the patron saint of friendship. Write down the names of your friends. As you do so, say a prayer for each one.

# Saint David the King

(c. 1000 BC)

Trust in God's **mercy** and **love!**

Feast Day
December
**29**

**David the King** was a shepherd boy when he was called by God to be king of Israel. It happened like this: The prophet Samuel came to his house, looking for the next king. Samuel asked to see each of David's seven brothers. As the brother were brought before him, Samuel rejected each one. Samuel asked David's father if he had any more sons. David's father replied that his youngest was watching the sheep.

As soon as David arrived, Samuel knew that David was God's chosen. He anointed David to become the next king. David was a good king who cared about his people. But he was not perfect. However, when he realized that he had sinned, he was truly sorry. He begged God's forgiveness, and God forgave him.

David wrote many psalms, and also played the lyre (a small harp). The psalm he wrote after God forgave his sin is Psalm 51, which begins, "Be merciful to me, O God, / because of your constant love." If we are sorry for our sins, we can count on God's mercy and love.

## Prayer

**Saint David the King**, pray for me, that I may trust in God's mercy and love.

God forgives our sins when we pray the "Lord, have mercy" at Mass, or when we pray the Our Father. But we are especially assured of God's forgiveness in the Sacrament of Penance and Reconciliation. When does your parish celebrate this sacrament? Write the times here. Make a plan to go together as a family.